of Supp̲... ̲ews'

*

GENERAL EDITOR
T. O. Beachcroft

WALTER DE LA MARE

WALTER
DE LA MARE

By KENNETH HOPKINS

'*What lovely things thy hand hath made*'

PUBLISHED FOR
THE BRITISH COUNCIL
and the NATIONAL BOOK LEAGUE
BY LONGMANS, GREEN & CO., LONDON, NEW YORK, TORONTO

LONGMANS, GREEN & CO. LTD.
6 & 7 Clifford Street, London, W,1
Also at Melbourne and Cape Town

LONGMANS, GREEN & CO. INC.
55 Fifth Avenue, New York, 3

LONGMANS, GREEN & CO.
215 Victoria Street, Toronto, 1

ORIENT LONGMANS LTD.
Bombay, Calcutta, Madras

First published in 1953

Printed in Great Britain by Benham and Company Limited
Colchester

CONTENTS

To W. J. de la M.

Friend, I have read your books and have written this ;
Partial, inadequate and brief it is,
But a reader, somewhere, may turn from my words to yours
Where profit and pleasure await him, and after, pause
Thinking of what I have written on what he has read :
' And everything left unsaid ! '

WALTER DE LA MARE

I

I T is more than fifty years since the quiet, consistent, and
magical voice of Walter de la Mare was first heard in
English poetry, and throughout those years he has given
us poetry that epitomizes the mystery and the evocative
loveliness of the written word; an essence of poetry, it may
seem, that has not been obviously affected by the violent
changes of the contemporary world. Yet to say this—even to
say he is a great lyric poet, with Campion, Blake, Shelley,
Landor, Bridges—is insufficient. Walter de la Mare cannot
be labelled in a sentence. The range and quantity of his work,
in verse and prose, is considerable; its uniform excellence is
remarkable, for he has never written a book, a paragraph,
or a word which was not the best he could do. No poet of
our time has commanded a purer or more spontaneous
initial inspiration, and none has brought to the aid of inspiration so cautious and deliberate a craftsmanship. 'Second
thoughts in everything are best, but in rhyme third and
fourth don't come amiss', says Byron. de la Mare has
achieved the marriage of craftsmanship with inspiration
without damaging either. Nowhere in his work is there any
element of the careless or the facile. The delicate art may be
conscious, but the unaltering integrity is inherent, con-
ditioning, and informing every chapter, every line.

The influence of such a writer on his contemporaries, and
on a younger generation, will not be small and cannot be
unfortunate. It is not dependent upon novelty, excess, or
fashion. It is not transitory. Increasingly, in these past years
his contemporaries have acknowledged it, his juniors have
profited by it; and to the general reader it has been a comfort
and a delight. For de la Mare—'a divine star of sweet wit and
invention'—has written always books which

> . . . have the charm
> Of visionary things, and lovely forms

And sweet sensations that throw back our life
And almost make our infancy itself
A visible scene, on which the sun is shining.

II

Walter de la Mare is not a writer whose works can best be read in the light of a background knowledge of his life. His adventures have not included shipwrecks, forest fires, or midnight alarums. His attachments have all been local : birds, clouds, the seasons; and his travels have not been to the sites of ancient battlefields, or to cities having the largest this, or the most celebrated that. H. M. Tomlinson recalls that years after a visit to Toledo Robert Lynd's best memory of the city was the glimpse he had there of a golden oreole. de la Mare is a traveller in this tradition. A sketch of his life will not be necessary for the appreciation of his works, but it may be desirable for other reasons. Such details have an interest apart from literary criticism.

Walter John de la Mare was born at Charlton, Kent, on 25 April 1873. His father, James Edward de la Mare, was of Huguenot descent, his mother was a Scot. He was educated at St. Paul's Cathedral Choir School and at sixteen entered the employment of the Anglo-American Oil Company at their London office. For nearly twenty years—until he was thirty-five—the Company's affairs were his daily concern, and literature only a sideline. But the boy who founded a magazine at school would not easily give up writing, and some of that writing began to appear in the magazines—in *Black and White*, *The Sketch*, *The Pall Mall Gazette*, and others. This was in the years immediately before 1900. In 1902 Longmans published *Songs of Childhood*, by Walter Ramal (the *nom de plume* which appeared again in 1904 on *Henry Brocken* and was then discarded). A poet working within the common tradition, but with something distinctive and individual to add to that tradition, is seldom recognized on his first appearance. Novelty is soon noticed,

iconoclasm is news; but the poet who is to make his way by
less spectacular methods must expect the way to be a long
one. *Songs of Childhood* 'numbered good intellects', but did
not make famous the name of Walter Ramal.

In 1908 de la Mare felt able to give up his office job and
devote himself to letters for a living. His reputation was small,
but it was increasing; and it was then relatively easier to live
as a free-lance writer than it is to-day when magazines and
newspapers are fewer, and space is restricted.

For the next thirty years de la Mare lived the life of a pro-
fessional man of letters: his books—prose and verse—appeared regularly, he contributed to the principal journals of
this country and the United States, he visited America to
lecture, and as the years passed he became himself the subject
of lectures. He has never 'retired' in the accepted sense (as I
write this he is engaged, in his eightieth year, in 'toiling over
a rhyme—for the young, too!'), but since the late war he has
lived somewhat in retirement, he is a rarer visitor at the
proceedings of learned societies, and his occasional writings
are fewer.

To summarize thus, in forty lines, a lifetime of eighty
years is manifestly absurd, and I have done so only because
a more extended biography is outside my present purpose.
As Forrest Reid said in his careful monograph on de la Mare,
'Such a biographical introduction as one may prefix to the
study of a living author's work is rarely of much significance.
His life is private, and if his readers are curious to learn about
his childhood, boyhood, and youth, he alone has a right to
gratify that interest.'

The warning has a particular pertinence to Walter de la
Mare because he has nowhere given any sustained autobiographical chapters, and even the occasional few
words of reminiscence dropped into an essay are usually
oblique enough to leave a doubt. The most careful
sifting of this evidence would not produce a true chapter
of his life.

III

For a critical survey it is usually convenient to divide a writer's work into its several kinds—prose, verse; fiction, non-fiction—but it must be remembered that such divisions are artificial. I shall consider de la Mare's work under such divisions, but the reader coming newly to it ought to read it all of a piece, for the several kinds illustrate and complement one another.

When *Songs of Childhood* was published in 1902 its author might have collected a small volume of short stories also, but it was in fact a long time before some of those earlier stories were reprinted, and others must still be read, if they are to be read at all, in the files of forgotten magazines. Instead, de la Mare's first prose work in book form was the romance—the 'completely inornate romance'—called *Henry Brocken* (1904).

This is one of several of de la Mare's books which come into no accepted category; *Ding Dong Bell* and *Desert Islands* and the highly individual anthologies with commentary are others. They are works entirely personal in approach, and to the merit of novelty must be added—in *Henry Brocken*—its disadvantages. Despite many charming passages, *Henry Brocken* is not a complete success.

Henry Brocken one day saddles his uncle's horse and rides away from home, leaving behind the memory of his dead parents, and of his Aunt Sophia's faded kindliness, and of his uncle's low, book-filled chamber. But Henry Brocken's journey is across hills that are not contemporary and his adventures are among people familiar enough in libraries, but not alive in the world—Lucy Gray, some girls of Herrick's, Jane Eyre, and Bottom the Weaver. The old horse Rosinante carries Henry down byways never before followed by living horse and rider.

The style of this early book is consciously archaic—at times rather self-consciously so. It abounds in words not in common use, and yet not exactly uncommon: probably it is the number of them, rather than any of them singly, that makes the prose seem faintly outmoded and only half awake. Except for one vivid passage, the whole work drifts like a dream.

Henry Brocken has come to the country of the Houyhnhnms, where he finds temporary shelter with one Lemuel Gulliver, whose Yahoo servant befriends him. It is necessary for him to leave, but he has become separated from Rosinante, and the Yahoo undertakes to guide him and carry him. The Houyhnhnms pursue with terrible tossing manes and polished hoofs. Then comes this splendid passage, as the Yahoo runs with Henry on his back and the horses at their heels:

> Two things grew clearer to me each instant. First, that every movement and feint of our pursuers was of design. Not a beast that wheeled but wheeled to purpose ; while the main body never swerved, thundered superbly on toward the inevitable end. And next, I perceived with even keener assurance that my guide knew his country and his enemy and his own power and aim as perfectly and consummately ; knew, too— this was the end.
>
> Far distant in front of us there appeared to be a break in the level green, a fringe of bushes, rougher ground. For this refuge he was making, and from this our mutinous Houyhnhnms meant to keep us. There was no pausing now, not a glance behind. His every effort was bent on speed. Speed indeed it was. The wind roared in my ears. Yet above its surge I heard the neighing and squealing, the ever-approaching shudder of hoofs. My eyes distorted all they looked on. I seemed now floating twenty feet in air ; now skimming within touch of the ground. Now that sorrel squadron behind me swelled and nodded ; now dwindled to an extreme minuteness of motion.
>
> Then, of a sudden, a last, shrill pæan rose high ; the hosts of our pursuers paused, billow-like, reared, and scattered—my poor Yahoo leapt clear.
>
> For an instant once again in this wild journey I was poised, as it were, in space, then fell with a crash, still clutched, sure and whole, to the broad shoulders of my rescuer.
>
> When my first confusion had passed away, I found that I was lying in a dense green glen at the foot of a cliff. For some

moments I could think of nothing but my extraordinary escape
from destruction. Within reach of my hand lay the creature
who had carried me, huddled and motionless ; and to left and
to right of me, and one a little nearer the base of the cliff, five
of those sorrel horses that had been chief of our pursuers. One
only of them was alive, and he, also, broken and unable to rise—
unable to do else than watch with fierce, untamed, glazing eyes
(a bloody froth at his muzzle) every movement and sign of life
that I made.

I myself, though bruised and bleeding, had received no serious
injury. But my Yahoo would rise no more. His master was
left alone amidst his people. I stooped over him and bathed
his brow and cheeks with the water that trickled from the cliffs
close at hand. I pushed back the thick strands of matted yellow
hair from his eyes. He made no sign. Even while I watched
him the life of the poor beast near at hand welled away : he
whinnied softly, and dropped his head upon the bracken. I
was alone in the unbroken silence.

Henry Brocken is full of detached beauties, but it is too in-
conclusive as a whole. More than fine writing is needed in a
narrative of two hundred pages, and it is perhaps because it
is on so much smaller a scale that the later *Ding Dong Bell* is
more effective. *Ding Dong Bell* (1924) consists of three[1]
essays, or sketches, or stories—call them what you will—
woven round a group of epitaphs. A woman, waiting on a
little country station for a train, enters into conversation
with an old man who shows her the curious stones in the
nearby graveyard and talks about the rhymes they bear;
two lovers, lost in the fields on a summer night come into a
deserted graveyard and puzzle out a few inscriptions by the
light of a handful of matches; a man lingers in a churchyard
on a cold January day and encounters—whom? or what? as
he reads over the inscriptions. The book makes less than
eighty pages, a subtle brief blending of exquisite verse and
prose, a collect for all who would muse upon death. The
little epitaphs themselves have not been taken from their

[1] Four in the latest edition, which includes ‘ Strangers and Pilgrims ’,
originally in the American edition of *The Wind Blows Over* (1936).

prose context for reprinting in the *Collected Poems*, and this is well, for the book is a perfect whole. See thus how the verses marry with the commentary:

> Cold and cheerless, we sat down once more to await the coming of the dawn. And it was the sun's first clear beams, putting to shame all remembrance of night, that, slanting in palest gold, lit up for us a little odd stone at our feet, almost hidden in brambles :

> > *Be very quiet now :*
> > *A child's asleep*
> > *In this small cradle,*
> > *In this shadow deep !*

> Words have strange capricious effects. *Now*, it was as if I could actually recall in memory itself the infant face in its white frilled cap—icily still, stonelike.

> And then I raised my eyes and looked into the living face of the living one beside me. Hers were fixed as if absently on the broken inscription, the curved lids fitting them as closely as its calix the rose. The face was cold and listless ; her hands idle in her lap. It was as though the beauty of her face were lying (like a mask) dead and forgotten, the self within was so far away.

> A thrush broke into song, as if from another world. Conscious at last of my silence perhaps, she slowly lifted her head into the gilding sunshine. And as if with a shrug of her slender shoulders, ' Now for the rest of our lives', she said.

In the years 1904–10, between the publication of *Henry Brocken* and *The Return*, de la Mare reached maturity as a writer of prose. In 1910 appeared two very different works, *The Three Mulla-Mulgars* and *The Return*: different, but with this much in common: both were stamped with a genius of which *Henry Brocken* had given only the promise.

IV

The Three Mulla-Mulgars—later renamed (I think unfortunately) *The Three Royal Monkeys*—is a story for children: not young children, but children from, say, ten to fourteen.

The adult reader ought not to overlook it on this account, for it contains some of de la Mare's most delicate writing.

The Three Mulla-Mulgars are three monkeys who are princes of their people, dispossessed and exiled. At the beginning of the story, their widowed mother dies and the three set out to find the land—far away—where reigns their Uncle Assasimmon. The book describes the hazards of the journey and their final success in reaching at last the desired haven: 'and there an end'. Into this comparatively uncomplicated plot the author introduces the subtlest under- and overtones of characterization and description. His three heroes, and especially the youngest, Nod, are (we feel) truly monkeys: they behave, react, think, and speak as monkeys should, with that small extra something which naturally would be added in royal blood. A comparison here with *The Jungle Book* is inevitable, but Kipling's animals although more realistic are somehow less credible. 'Look well, O Wolves!' is theatrically effective, but under scrutiny it does not appear true; and indeed the *Just So Stories* come nearer than the *Jungle Books* to de la Mare's romance, but without his persuasive magic. Absorbing and at times exciting as the story is, it is in the writing itself that *The Three Mulla-Mulgars* is most rewarding; like *Henry Brocken* before it, but more maturely, it gives us a remarkable exercise in sustained poetic prose.

> Night began to fall, and the long-beaked bats to flit in their leathery hoods, seeking small birds and beasts to quench their thirst. It seemed now to Nod, his brave heart fallen, that he was utterly forsaken. Darkness had always sent him scuttling home to the Portingal's hut when he was little. How often his mother had told him that Noomanossi with his luring harp-strings roamed these farther forests, and strange beasts, too, that never show their faces to the sun ! Worse still, as he lifted his poor wrinkled forehead to the tree-tops to catch the last beams of day, he felt a dreadful presence around him. Leopard it was not, nor Gunga, nor Minimul.
>
> He stood still, his left hand resting on its knuckles in the snow,

his right clutching his cudgel, and leaning his round ear side-
long, he listened and listened. He put down his cudgel, and
stood upright, his hands clasped behind his neck, and lifting his
flat nose, sniffed and sniffed again the scarcely-stirring air.
There was a smell, faint and strange. He turned as if to rush
away, to hide himself—anywhere away from this brooding,
terrifying smell, when, as if it were a little voice speaking
beneath his ribs, he heard the words : ' Fear not, Ummanodda ;
press on, press on ! '

He took up his cudgel with a groan, and limped quickly
forward, and in an instant before he could start back, before
even he could cry out, he heard a click, his foot slipped, out of
the leaves whipped something smooth and shining, and he was
jerked into the air, caught, bound fast in a snare.

He writhed and kicked, he spat and hissed. But the more
he struggled, the tighter drew the cord round his neck. Everywhere, faint and trembling, rose the strange and dreadful un-
known smell. He hung quite still. And as he dangled in pain,
a night-wandering Bittock on a branch above him called
piteously : ' Oo-ee, oo-ee, oo-ee ! '

' Why do you mock me, my friend ? ' groaned Nod.

' Oo-ee, oo-ee, oo-ee ! ' wailed the Bittock, and hopping slowly
down, perched herself before his face. Her black eye gleamed.
She clapped her tiny wings above her head, and slowly let them
fold. ' Oo-ee, oo-ee, oo-ee ! ' she cried again.

Nod stared in a rage : ' Oo-ee, oo-ee ! ' he mocked her feebly.
' Who's caught me in this trap ? Why do you come mocking
me, swinging here to die ? Put out my eyes, Bird of Sorrow.
Nod's tired of being Nod.'

The little bird seemed to listen, with rusty poll poked forward.
She puffed out her feathers, raised her pointed bill, and
piercingly into the shadows rang out her trembling voice again.
' Oo-ee, oo-ee, oo-ee ! ' she sang, spread her wings, and left Nod
quite alone.

His thong twitched softly. He shut his eyes. And once
again, borne on the faint cold wind, that smell came sluggishly
to his nostrils. His fears boiled up. His hair grew wet on his
head. And suddenly he heard a distant footfall. Nearer and
nearer—not panther's, nor Gunga's, nor Ephelanto's. And
then some ancient voice whispered in his memory : ' Oomgar,
Oomgar ! ' Man !

These early prose works all show, in different ways, the mark of a writer with great gifts not yet fully under control; we feel in *Henry Brocken* that the narrative takes the writer along paths of its own choosing, rather than those he intends; some of the early stories are exercises, trials of strength: and why not? For only so can a writer develop and come to perfection. *The Three Mulla-Mulgars* in another way reveals this conflict between the writer and his writing, for it is a work without a distinct purpose. If it is a children's story—and certainly the author read it to his children—then why is so much of it in manner and content beyond the immediate appreciation of children? On the other hand, if it is not a children's story, what is it? What comment did it evoke from the young listeners who heard it first?

The last of those early prose works is *The Return*. It is the most successful. It is at once clear what particular niche it fills, for it is obviously a novel; it has a recognizable theme, is clearly divided into chapters, the story begins, develops and ends. At last—de la Mare's readers might have said—this writer has set himself a clearly defined task, and gone ahead with it.

In *The Return* the hero, Arthur Lawford, a sensitive, rather indecisive man, given more to introspection than action, falls asleep in a churchyard near the grave of a suicide. While he sleeps the spirit of the suicide tries to take possession of his body: and to some extent succeeds. Thereafter, in subtle and disturbing prose, we are given the story of Lawford's struggle against the adversary within—a struggle almost wholly private and withheld and yet as terrible as any clash of arms, and with Lawford beset too by the uncomprehension of his wife and perhaps most of all by the consciousness of being essentially alone. He finds the only outside help that comes to him in the house and presence of a brother and sister living near the churchyard, and his own best effort in his love for his young daughter. None of these people can help actively—indeed, some of them, his wife and ordinary circle of friends, are hardly conscious of the struggle except by the change in his manner, and the failing of his health—and the force that finally overcomes the unquiet intruder is mainly Lawford's own, though sustained by the love and understanding of Grisel, the tolerance of her brother Herbert, and his desperate love for Alice his daughter.

This story might have been something like *Dr. Jekyll and Mr. Hyde*; or it might have had the throbbing horror found in such stories by Kipling as *At the End of the Passage* and *In the Same Boat*; again, it might have followed the precedent of Lord Lytton's *The Haunted and The Haunters*, with all of which it has points superficially in common—as a theme. But in the event *The Return* is more dissimilar to all these works than similar. The supernatural is perhaps the least important part of it, once the initial 'haunting' has occurred; the intense spiritual conflict that follows might equally well have been between opposing aspects of the man's own soul (as Jekyll and Hyde), between the man and some monstrous figment of disease and fantasy (as in the two Kipling stories), or even between the man and huge, horrible and impersonal forces, as in Lytton. So far a parallel might go, but thereafter, because de la Mare is so little influenced by others, or rather, perhaps, because he is so individual a writer, it breaks and becomes irrelevant. *The Return* is a religious book, even though 'religion' is not one of the greatest of Lawford's helps in adversity. It is religious, because it expresses the belief that even an ordinary rather weak and puzzled man, can enter into a contest with evil—evil backed by all the age-old resources of success in a prospering trade—and still against all the odds prevail.

V

In the years 1902–21 de la Mare's output, book for book, was more in verse than in prose; a dozen volumes of verse may be set beside only half a dozen in prose. To anyone assessing his position at the end of twenty years active authorship he must have seemed to be chiefly a poet. This was not strictly true. For during those years, much reviewing and other journalism apart, de la Mare was quietly accumulating a body of short stories which have always seemed to me strangely undervalued. By 'undervalued' I don't mean ignored; they have been widely read, widely praised, and frequently reprinted. But I think there is more to be said than this, for these stories are among the fines. the last fifty years have produced.

The earliest of them appeared in print even longer ago than that; the latest—I hope is yet to come. Sixty years and more have produced sixty stories, and more. This underlines an important point: these stories were not hastily written, were not 'magazine stories' produced in a hurry for ready money and fit only for an ephemeral purpose. Each, whether wholly or only partly 'successful, is as much a piece of art as any of the author's lyrics; and indeed, allowing for the difference in medium and in the approach dictated by that medium, each is in effect a poem. It has the form necessitated by its nature, and it has its own integrity. It is written not because such a length, such a plot, was 'marketable', but because only in that special way could this special thing be treated. Thus these stories record atmosphere and mood; exquisite and delicate relationships, and the most tenuous and precise shades of meaning, and they do this as much by what is withheld as by what is expressed. For in nothing save poetry itself, is selection so difficult, or so necessary.

The short stories, more than any other part of de la Mare's large and varied literary baggage, are complementary to the poems ; the stories comment upon, amplify, underline the poems; and the poems, time and again, give that flash of illumination which makes instantaneously clear a whole tangled landscape of thought. *The Riddle*, for example— one of the shortest of the stories, one of the simplest in language, is one of the least ' clear '. Seven children come to live with their grandmother, who bids them be happy and play where they will—except that they must not play in the large spare bedroom in which stands a great old oak chest. The children settle down and live quietly and pleasantly ; but as time passes now one, now another forgets or ignores the warning, until at last all have ventured into the old chest and vanished. There is not one riddle here, but many ; and at the third, the fifth reading, the whole implication has not been exhausted. It is too simple to say that the author has embroidered the theme of Haynes Bayly's ballad of 'The Mistletoe Bough'. The tragedy there was sad enough, but perfectly simple ; whereas in *The Riddle* it is not even easy to say where the tragedy lies. The children vanish so utterly and irrevocably that one is tempted to wonder whether they ever existed ; whether, in fact, the tragedy does not centre wholly in the old lady, with her mind 'a tangled skein of memories—laughter and tears, and little children now old-fashioned, and the advent of friends, and long farewells. . . .'

For a strange, breathless, and disquieting comment on the riddle in this story read that other riddle, the poem 'The Feckless Dinner Party'. The two works take colour from one another ; lend one another new significance ; but, of course, do not 'explain'. For to explain would be to destroy.

It is always true to say that a writer's work is 'all of a piece', whatever its form, in that it derives from a single mind ; but this becomes a central canon of criticism in assessing the work of de la Mare. *The Riddle* and 'The Feckless Dinner Party' exemplify the point. The story is a poetic conception ; though it is without metre and rhyme, his execution approaches poetry. The poem, on the other hand, might have taken the form of a short story—that is to say, a short story by de la Mare.

The stories and the poems of de la Mare follow the same threads of thought, the same lines of argument. They treat of children, old ladies, ghosts felt but seldom seen, tragedies so personal and so long ago that none but the narrator recalls them ; in the telling are the same distant, clouded landscapes, the same tenuous perfumes, the same faded pictures, tapestries, cloths.   These few sentences from *The Green Room* epitomize the deceptively undemonstrative style of the stories, a style wonderfully evocative of old, gracious times and lovely things but with power to disturb where violence would be ineffective:

> So Alan proceeded on his way.   The drugget on the passage floor showed little trace of wear.   The low panelled walls had been white-washed.   He came at last to the flowered china handle of the door beyond the turn of the passage, then stood for a moment lost in surprise.   But it was the trim cobbled garden beyond the square window on his right that took his glance rather than the room itself.   Yellow crocuses, laden with saffron pollen, stood wide agape in the black mould, and the greening buds of a bush of lilac were tapping softly against the glass.   And above was a sky of the gentlest silken blue ; wonderfully still.
>
> He turned and looked about him.   The paint on wainscot and cornice must once have been of a bright apple green.   It had faded now.   A gate-leg table was in the far corner beyond the small-paned window ; and on his left, with three shallow steps up to it, was another door.   And the shelves were lined from floor to ceiling with the literary treasures which Mr. Elliott kept solely for his elect.   So quiet was the room that even the flitting of a clothes-moth might be audible, though the brightness of noonday now filled it to the brim.   For the three poplars beyond the lilac bush were still almost as bare as the frosts of winter had made them.

Such writing as this—and hundreds of similar passages might be quoted—has the visual quality of a Vermeer painting : indeed, from it a painting could be made, and not only of what is described.   For the house, even the town are implied.   The window is ' square ' and (later) ' small-paned ' ; the cobbled garden is ' trim ' ; the passage is ' panelled '.   The room is very quiet.   There are three steps out of it.   It has ' flowered-china door handles '. These details, cumulatively—with the pale faded paint, even the ' gate-leg ' table—suggest a Georgian house in a country town, little altered for a hundred years.   In that March silence, clear and chilly, one almost expects to hear an abbey tower sprinkling the quarters from ancient bells.

It is a perfect setting, so delicately sketched, for the delicate ghost, herself no more than a sketch but wonderfully ' like ', who is to appear so soon with her demands upon Alan.

The Green Room is typical of de la Mare's ghost stories ; those ghost stories in which the last thing looked for or given is an ' explanation ' and in which the very ghost itself is often enough rather hinted at than seen.   de la Mare's ghosts are the least substantial of our time, though they have some affinity with those of Oliver Onions.   Beside them, the wraiths of M. R. James, of W. W. Jacobs, of May Sinclair, seem very much ' alive ', more positive in action and more solid in physical shape.   ' The petrifaction of a sigh ' ? —de la Mare would know something about that.

They are ghostly enough, these ghosts of de la Mare's ; sometimes almost imperceptibly tenuous ; but they have the same power to terrify, and perhaps more.   In *The Ash-Tree* by M. R. James we expect violence ; for it was by violence that Sir Matthew Fell called retribution down upon himself and his house—and it is the same in W. W. Jacobs' *The Monkey's Paw*, and many other familiar stories.   In de la Mare that initial violence that provokes revenge—' even from beyond the grave '—is usually lacking.   His ghosts come not to kill, but to trouble.   Their stories are not less effective because they are not stained with blood.

In *The House*, for example, the ghost is real enough, but friendly rather than otherwise, although with no special cause.   She takes the wallet (not for the first time ?) and vanishes.   No recriminations, no ' haunting '.   In *A Recluse* the eccentric Mr. Bloom is perhaps less happy than his rather effusive cheerfulness suggests ; and he has cause to be. But even he comes to no special harm in the story itself, whatever fate we are left expecting to befall him.

For, horrible moments though there are in the stories that touch on aspects of the supernatural, it is in his stories of ' ordinary ' men and women—and children—that de la Mare gives us the most sustained and effective of his horrors. *In the Forest* is an example : the events in it are tragic, and the boy's character is most unsympathetic, for what he does and for the ignoble motives that prompt him. He is utterly insensitive, one would say : and yet . . . how far were his actions dictated by loneliness, the drawbacks of upbringing and environment, the special circumstances of the times, the absence of his father . . . all of which serve to explain, if not to excuse his conduct ? However, we see the tragedy, as it happened ; and as it had to happen because the boy was what he was. It is all told from the boy's point of view, without a false note.

The father has gone to war—a civil war, with fighting but a few miles from the house—leaving the boy with his mother and a sick baby. The boy gives his mother no help ; he prefers going fishing to fetching the doctor. The baby dies. The mother then takes the body of the baby to the village for burial, leaving the boy to watch the house ; while she is away the father returns, wounded. The last paragraphs have a finality more effective than any recorded emotion : they are matter-of-fact enough, but how terrible the fact itself is is graphically brought home : the story has the intense concentrated force of Saki's *Sredni Vashtar* in its somewhat different way, or of Kipling's *Mary Postgate*.

> I fell asleep unawares. When I awoke it was broad daylight. I felt very glad and relieved to see the light, even though mother had not come back. It seemed to me that some noise had awakened me. Presently there came a groan at the doorway. Kneeling down and peeping through a crevice between the planks, I saw my father lying there on the doorstep. I took down the bar and opened the door. He was lying on his stomach ; his clothes were filthy and torn, and at the back of his shoulder was a small hole pushed in in the cloth. There was dark, thick blood on the withered leaves. I tried to see his

face, but couldn't very well. It was all muddy, bleared and
white, and he groaned and swore when I touched him. But
he didn't know who I was, and some of what he said didn't
seem to me to have any sense.

He asked for some water, but I could not turn him over so
that he could drink it. And it was all spilt. I told him about
the baby dying, but he didn't show that he could hear anything ;
and just as I finished I heard mother coming back from the
churchyard. So I ran out and told her that it was father.

In the Forest is fine as a study of a child's outlook, but it is
not so fine as *The Almond Tree*, in which a broken marriage
is described by a child who scarcely understands the implications of the things he has seen : ' They have put my father
in the little parlour, in his coffin ; of course, you know he's
dead, and Mrs. Marshall's come ; she gave me a ha'penny
this morning. Dr. Graham gave me a whole crown,
though.' These are but two of a whole group of studies
of children, some told by the child itself, and others by an
independent observer. Of these, perhaps the finest is
The Trumpet, a magnificent short story which I might be
tempted to think de la Mare's greatest if so many other
contending titles did not at once spring to mind. . . .

All these stories have certain things in common : neither
in treatment nor theme do they vary much and—always—
it is the people and how they react that is important. What
happens matters little, except for the effect it has on character ; and in some of the stories nothing very much does
happen. In others, things happen ' off-stage ' ; or have
happened ' a long time ago '.

Childhood, old age ; the tales of an old eccentric ; the
story of a picture, a work of art, an old house, a legacy—
these are the themes. And love, about which every writer
must write : de la Mare approaches love almost always
obliquely : if his characters kiss, he seldom tells.

But, with his delicate insight, it is inevitable that such love
stories as he does write are things of rare beauty. The
wistful passages in *The Talisman*, the strange, pathetic love

of *At First Sight*, and the moving account of Mr. Anon's
devotion to Miss M., in *Memoirs of a Midget*.

Memoirs of a Midget is his most sustained piece of prose
fiction, an astonishing piece of virtuosity, for this ' auto-
biography ' of a midget is always perfectly credible and
' in key ' ; indeed, the smallness of Miss M. is conveyed as
surely, and more delicately, even than the smallness of
Gulliver among the Brobdingnagians, or of the Lilliputians
beside Gulliver. Swift uses the matter-of-fact reporters'
method which Kipling later found so effective. de la
Mare is more oblique ; he suggests, implies, and seldom
makes a direct statement : but that Miss M. is very small
indeed is never in doubt. The mastery, however, is not
simply in suggesting a very tiny person among ordinary
people. It is in herself, her character, her reactions : she
' thinks small '. Her outlook, her reactions, are always
' small '. It is as though the writer, before commencing
his task, had taken a draught from that magical bottle in
Alice's Adventures in Wonderland and reduced himself to the
scale of his heroine.

There is no book by de la Mare less easy to ' discuss ',
for—as with a poem (and once more we are reminded how
closely poet and prose writer join in de la Mare)—the work
is its own interpretation. A quotation would give some
idea of the beauty of the writing, and a synopsis of the plot
would give—just that. But these would give no real
indication of this work, unique in conception and virtually
flawless in execution. It is the triumphant justification
of *Henry Brocken*.

VI

To say de la Mare writes ' a poet's prose ' might do him a
disservice, for the phrase sometimes suggests the whimsical,
even the effeminate. But although in de la Mare there is a
good deal of fanciful, elaborate, or even mannered writing, he
is capable of prose as direct and simple as that of Dryden. This
may be sufficiently demonstrated by reference to his essays.

The essays take several forms, and are all more or less
' occasional '. They occur as introductions to books—his
own, or those of other writers—as contributions to sym-
posia, as lectures reprinted, as long critical reviews. Of
essays written simply as such, and so published, there are few.
The long *Desert Islands* is the most important of these.
Most of the rest come into the categories first mentioned—
but they are none the worse for that. And they afford an
impressive body of critical prose quite separate from the
prose of the tales.

In *Pleasures and Speculations* (1940) the author gathered a
dozen of these essays and *Private View* (for publication in
1953) contains a further gathering almost wholly of reviews.
These, if the reader adds the long introductions to *Love*,
and *Behold, This Dreamer*, *Desert Islands* and *Early One
Morning* make a readily accessible collection as necessary
to the understanding of de la Mare's work as the other prose.

To say ' introductions ' in speaking of the prose commentaries in *Love* and *Behold, This Dreamer* is misleading. These
anthologies are full examinations of their subjects (I don't
say ' final ') and in both cases the introduction is well over a
hundred pages long ; the anthology is as much a commentary on the introduction as the introduction is on the
anthology. These two works are more nearly conventional
anthologies, in that the chosen pieces are grouped separately
from the commentary, than the third, *Early One Morning*.
In this the quotations and citations are blended with the
commentary ; are sometimes paraphrased ; sometimes,
indeed, are ' digested ' into the writer's own ; so that at
first sight the whole long book appears to be ' de la Mare on
children and childhood '. A glance at the index disproves
this impression : it seems, indeed, that he has gathered
thoughts, memories, glimpses of childhood from every
writer of standing in the past twenty centuries. de la Mare
looks for his material in the life of Al Capone, or the writings
of the learned Sir William Jones. Indeed, as these three
anthologies, and the other, *Come Hither*, amply demonstrate,

the range of de la Mare's reading is prodigious. He seems to have read everything. In *Come Hither*, a ' collection of rhymes and poems for the young of all ages', there are nearly five hundred poems from three hundred writers ; and he finds ' rhymes for the young ' in Wolcot, Lydgate, and Alexander Scott. In *Love* he quotes nearly three hundred writers, including writers on this subject as apparently unrewarding as Erasmus Darwin.

His range as a critic can well be indicated by a few titles : *The Early Novels of Wilkie Collins*, *Rupert Brooke and the Intellectual Imagination*, *Poetry in Prose*, *Flowers and Poetry*, *Lewis Carroll*, *Tennyson*. His Warton Lecture, *Poetry in Prose* (1935) delivered before the British Academy, is an interesting contribution to the study of English prosody, for it discusses how far ' poetry ' can enter into ' prose '.

VII

The reader approaching de la Mare's poetry for the first time will find the bulk of it in six volumes. *Collected Poems*, which contains an almost complete gathering of the poems published up to 1942 ; *Collected Rhymes and Verses*, which contains most of the children's and light verse published up to 1944 ; two later collections of lyrics, *The Burning Glass* (1945) and *Inward Companion* (1950) ; and two long lyrical poems, *The Traveller* (1946) and *Winged Chariot* (1951). This body of work affords rather more than eight hundred short lyrics averaging about twenty-four lines each, and the two longer lyrics published separately. One warning must be given before the reader embarks upon the *Collected Rhymes and Verses*. Do not suppose this title to mean a volume of amusing and unimportant trifles not strong enough for the companion *Collected Poems* ; for *Collected Rhymes* contains some of de la Mare's finest, and most characteristic, work.

Walter de la Mare is the supreme English lyric poet of our time and one of the great masters of the short lyric in English,

as truly a master as were Campion, Herrick, Herbert,
Landor, and Bridges before him ; a master, moreover, in
the same tradition that was theirs, of saying the perfect thing
in perfect form and language. This, for example, is as
final and unanswerable as the circle drawn by Apelles :

The Chart

That grave small face, but twelve hours here,
Maps secrets stranger than the seas',
In hieroglyphics more austere,
And older far than Rameses'.

That is one mood, a very common one in this poet, in
which a question is asked, or implied ; and a line of thought
is indicated along which the reader may then pursue his own
way. The initial impulse often, if not always, is one the reader
might not have come upon for himself, but once started
by the poet's help a world of speculation opens before him :

. . . no man knows
Through what wild centuries
Roves back the rose . . .

So, with a few words, lovely in themselves, he can conjure
up thoughts and memories even lovelier for being wordless.
' A music so remote and sweet it all but lovely as silence
is. . . .'
His utterance is sometimes deceptively quiet, deceptively
undemonstrative. The effect is often cumulative ; line by
line, stanza by stanza—even in a twenty-line poem—the
essential development proceeds unsuspected but inevitable.
Such a poem, for example, as ' Nod ', can be learned by
heart, can become a permanent part of one's consciousness,
yet never lose its magic.

' Nod '

Softly along the road of evening,
In a twilight dim with rose,
Wrinkled with age, and drenched with dew,
Old Nod, the shepherd, goes.

His drowsy flock streams on before him,
    Their fleeces charged with gold,
To where the sun's last beam leans low
    On Nod the shepherd's fold.

The Hedge is quick and green with briar,
    From their sand the conies creep ;
And all the birds that fly in heaven
    Flock singing home to sleep

His lambs outnumber a noon's roses,
    Yet, when night's shadows fall,
His blind old sheep-dog, Slumber-soon,
    Misses not one of all.

His are the quiet steeps of dreamland,
    The waters of no-more-pain,
His ram's bell rings 'neath an arch of stars,
    ' Rest, rest, and rest again.'

' Nod's ' effect I think is achieved in several ways. It begins rather conventionally, with ordinary phrases ' road of evening ', ' dim with rose ', such as anybody might write ; but in the second and third stanzas the verse begins to be beyond ' anybody's ' powers : the phrases ' streams on' and ' leans low ' with the particular rhythm which their use in that context creates, lifts the poem at once above its conventional beginning, and the subtle rhythm of the fourth stanza illustrates de la Mare's extraordinary mastery of the common four-line stanza. The key of the poem does not change as it develops, but the tone gathers intensity. The verse becomes more individual, and the use of rather archaic words increases its effect. ' Anybody ' could have begun this poem ; only de la Mare could have completed it.

The same may be said of scores of other lyrics ; he is never afraid of the conventional or ' poetic ' word or phrase if that best suits his need ; but he is able by mingling the familiar with the unexpected to heighten the value of both. ' The poet is to deal with the commonplace ', says George Saintsbury, ' and make it *not common*'. This de la Mare does. The sentiment in ' Nod ', and in a hundred others, may seem commonplace ; the result is ' not common '.

Nod, in fact, reveals a distinctive aspect of de la Mare's poetic character that may be traced in many of his lyrics. While he is evoking with delicate skill an apparently familiar landscape of the poetic world, another image appears behind it more remote, less known to humanity and at times charged with fear. The first image may be miniature, graceful, well known, the other is cold and giant like, drawn from impersonal worlds, where a single human conscious- ness is no more than a momentary affair. In many of the earlier lyrics we may feel this second world appears only as a hint or a question. In his recent long poem *The Traveller* the second world is in the foreground.

I do not suggest, of course, that the sentiment is always commonplace ; for a hundred lyrics with a conventional theme one might find another hundred with an original and ' de la Marian ' inspiration, for de la Mare looks at the world with inquiring and unprejudiced eyes and he sees things—as a poet should—for the ' first time ' no matter how many poets have seen them before him. That is why his titles at first reading seem unadventurous enough : ' Evening ', ' Dawn ', ' Age ', ' The Dreamer ', ' A Child Asleep ', ' Winter Dusk ', subjects ' rubbed by a hundred rhymsters, battered a thousand times '. It makes no difference, for these subjects are the stuff of human life and experience and he comes to them—despite his vast reading in the world's poetry—with the innocence of a child. To him they are new, and the poems he makes from them are new. Even his occasional ' echoes ' indicate merely an affinity, natural and unconscious, with Poe, or Burns, or Landor, or Shakespeare. There is no ' world of Walter de la Mare ', peopled with fairies and children ; he is squarely in the same world as the rest of us, but he sees deeper and further into its implications and even of the tangible and visible he sees more, or ' sees it more abun- dantly '.

de la Mare is often profoundly melancholy. The sense
of tragedy and mischance is never far away, and occurs, often
enough, in poems apparently light-hearted and small.
Consider this :

Hi !

Hi ! handsome hunting man
Fire your little gun.
Bang !   Now the animal
Is dead and dumb and done.
Nevermore to peep again, creep again, leap again,
Eat or sleep or drink again, Oh, what fun !

No ' inconscient happiness ' here ; but a pity and awareness
of the true nature of life.

de la Mare's sympathy with and understanding of animals
is one of his strongest characteristics ; it is found in a number
of the stories for children, in his gentle sketch of the horse
Rosinante in *Henry Brocken* (and in a few sentences among
those I have quoted, in which he glances with pity at the
broken Houyhnhnms) ; it fills *The Three Mulla-Mulgars* ; is
found—often in no more than a sentence—everywhere
among the other stories ; and of course makes a large part
of the complete poems. These animals always have dignity
and integrity ; are themselves, and true to themselves. He
never pokes fun at them, never dresses them up and sets
them capering. Instead, he speaks as a friend, defends and
protects them, wishes them well. Such a poem as ' Nicholas
Nye ' is much more than five verses about a donkey ; it is
a remarkable character sketch and more essentially so than
(for example) the theatrical figure in G. K. Chesterton's
famous poem, ' The Donkey ' :

. . . Fools ! for I also had my hour,
One far fierce hour and sweet ;
There was a shout about my ears
And palms before my feet. . . .

These are not the thoughts of Nicholas Nye, 'lame of a leg and old', as he stood in the meadow :

> *Alone with his shadow he'd drowse in the meadow,*
> *Lazily swinging his tail,*
> *At break of day he used to bray,—*
> *Not much too hearty and hale ;*
> *But a wonderful gumption was under his skin,*
> *And a clear calm light in his eye,*
> *And once in a while : he'd smile . . .*
> *Would Nicholas Nye.*

Nicholas Nye, and the others, are *true*—even the fish in the frying-pan that pauses from his sizzling to say ' Alack ! ' Birds, beasts, even insects have a spokesman in de la Mare, a spokesman unsentimental but sincere.

Animals, flowers, the seasons, the single uncomplicated emotions of fear, hunger, desire, these are his themes often enough ; and always to what we have heard before he will add the twist, or bring the extra insight, which stamps even the shortest of his poems with the unmistakable signature of its author. For de la Mare is a poet working within a conventional tradition whose genius is not for flamboyant disregard of the rules, but for triumphant conformity with them. He has not been obscure because he has not been a leader in the ' new ' and the revolutionary. It is not easy to find new things to say in poetry, or to say the old things freshly. But genius can be flexible enough to accommodate itself to tradition.

VIII

In 1902 de la Mare published *Songs of Childhood* (by ' Walter Ramal ') ; in 1950 he published *Inward Companion* ; and in the fifty years between he published a couple of dozen other collections, including such familiar titles as *The Listeners* (1912), *Peacock Pie* (1913), *Motley* (1918), *The Veil* (1921), *The Fleeting* (1933), and *Memory* (1938). These, with the post-war collections *The Burning-Glass*

(1945) and *Inward Companion* ought at first sight to give a far view of his development ; but it isn't so simple as that. A note in *Inward Companion* sounds the warning : ' One or two of the poems in the following collection were written as many as fifty years ago ; others during the last few years, and most of these are recent. All of them have been revised.'

Let the reader who is fond of puzzles read right through the book and then say which poems are fifty years old. This poet has indeed ' developed '—for what writer of genius stands still ?—but the development is not merely a matter of increasing skill, increasing subtlety of thought, or range of interest. The other warning given above is also relevant : ' All of them have been revised.'

The process of revision can occasionally be seen at work in de la Mare, for with successive reappearances of certain lyrics, first in book-form from magazines, then in ' collected ' volumes, slight verbal changes may be noted. These are refinements technically ; but to what extent do they damage the original spontaneity? It is a question every reader will answer for himself. I confess my own inclination is almost always for the earlier of successive versions, and occasionally the author comes at last to the same conclusion : there is a poem, ' Sleepyhead ', which Forrest Reid discusses at some length in his excellent study of de la Mare, tracing its mutations through several reprintings and concluding that the latest version is the least effective. This was in 1929. By the time the *Collected Rhymes and Verses* appeared in 1944 the poem had returned to its first form. This is an example of critical revision coming full circle ; in a full-length critical study it would be of interest to follow thus the fortunes of a number of the poems, but in this short essay it must suffice to indicate this as one more possible approach to the enjoyment of de la Mare's work.

For, like all the great poets, de la Mare can be lived with ; taken in short passages, he gives refreshment ; in extended reading he gives counsel and comfort. Before all else, he is to be read for pleasure ; and few living poets can give greater pleasure. He is to be read for the marvel of technique to be found in his verse and the variety of his music. He shows almost every excellence of which the four-line stanza in English is capable—and what a wealth of excellence that is.

The ' Georgian Poets' were as different from one another as were the Lake Poets, but (although the group is not greatly in fashion) between them they wrote much of the finest poetry of this century. Four of them—W. H. Davies, Wilfrid Gibson, Edmund Blunden, and Walter de la Mare—consistently used the common four-line stanza in ' eights' and ' sixes', or variations of it, and produced an astonishing range of effects. Here are a few examples, all from de la Mare, showing the subtle variations of time and rhythm obtainable without sacrifice of conventional form :

> A bird flies up from the hayfield ;
> Sweet, to distraction, is the new-mown grass :
> But I grieve for its flowers laid low at noonday—
> And only this poor Alas !

> If I had a drop of attar
> And a clot of wizard clay,
> Birds we would be with wings of light
> And fly to Cathay.

.   .   .

> Here lies, but seven years old, our little maid,
> Once of the darkness Oh, so sore afraid !
> Light of the World—remember that small fear,
> And when nor moon nor stars do shine, draw near !

IX

In 1946, without much preliminary flourish beyond the customary announcement in a publisher's list, appeared *The Traveller*, an entirely new manifestation of de la Mare's genius. He had written a long metaphysical and

'autobiographical' poem—seven hundred or so lines—
broken into four-line stanzas rhyming a–b, a–b with ten
syllable lines. And the first thing—its merit apart—that the
reader might notice is that, even in so long a poem, there is
no monotony. At the age of seventy-three this poet was
master of his instrument : indeed, *The Traveller* demon-
strates the incalculable value of 'experience'. Fifty years of
writing verse were behind it and it was technically im-
peccable.[1] But it takes more than this to make a poem ;
more than this—much more—*The Traveller* has.

A Traveller and his horse journey across a strange land
towards death, and come to death at last ; it is as much a
spiritual as a physical journey. When the poem begins
they are already nearing their journey's end ; indeed, in this
and other particulars there are affinities with the opening of
The Testament of Beauty. de la Mare's is the shorter, the
less ambitious poem, but it is equally packed with thought.
It is also full of pictures—pictures which make unnecessary,
to my mind, those that accompany the text.

> *On, and still on he pressed—scorched heel to nape,*
> *Hunched in his saddle from the noonday's glare—*
> *Watched by a winged thing, high in heaven, agape*
> *To ken aught stirring in a tract so bare.*
>
> *Which leaf or blade of grass could never yield.*
> *A vitreous region, like a sea asleep,*
> *Crystalline, convex, tideless and congealed,*
> *Profounder far than Tuscarora Deep,*
>
> *Further than sight could reach, before him lay.*

It is full, too, of brave reflection, of faith and courage, so

---

[1] Miss V. Sackville-West has pointed out small blemishes (*Tribute to
Walter de la Mare*, 1948), but I feel that what I have said is none-the-less
true ; an undoubted blemish in a ten-line lyric takes a different perspective
in seven hundred lines. In January 1953, Miss Sackville-West returned
to the subject in her Warton Lecture, ' Walter de la Mare and " The
Traveller " ', delivered before the British Academy.

that although the poem ends with death, we read into that
conclusion the hope of a new beginning.   And, throughout,
the lines of thought sketched in, for the reader to ' regard
or disregard ' :

> Even the little ant, devoid of fear,
>   Prowling beneath the shadow of a man,
> Conscious may be of occult puissance near,
>   Whose origin it neither recks, nor can.
>
> So, though he too was now but vaguely aware
>   Whence welled this boon of benison and peace,
> In awe of a mystery so divinely fair,
>   Tears gushed within him, not of grief but bliss.

The Traveller was a remarkable poem and a sufficient testi-
mony that Walter de la Mare does not come within William
Cory's definition

> . . . one's feelings lose poetic flow
> Soon after twenty-seven or so !

Yet there was still to come a work of astonishing richness,
Winged Chariot, published in 1951.

Description cannot do justice to *Winged Chariot* and
quotation, however chosen, will leave unquoted loveliness
as rare.   The impression is that the poet has thought end-
lessly about Time, read about Time, and given us a poet's
commonplace book with Time for theme and with each
aspect of it hinted at rather than explained.

> . . . Jasmine, and hyacinth, the briar rose
> Steep with their presence a whole night ; nor close :
> Time with an infinite gentleness through them flows.

The poem is broken into irregular lengths, mainly in
three-line, ten syllable stanzas, with occasional longer
passages, longer stanzas, and some few in a shorter, hurrying
measure : all in keeping with intractible, wilful Time.

Winged Chariot is by turns lyric, elegiac, meditative ; at moments it approaches the conversational though never the flaccid ; it has wit and dignity as well as passion.   All these moods are fused together in the unmistakable colours of de la Mare's genius.   The reader will feel delight that this deeper magic can spring to life with so much freshness.   Yet if we say that *Winged Chariot* is a crowning achievement, a harmony of all that de la Mare has been, we must notice also an added strength of thought : the maintenance through his images and visions of a discussion.   At times it seems that this poem is about to explain what lies behind the vanishing overtones and mysteries of the lyrics : but, although de la Mare may show his mature perception of many long tracts of metaphysical argument, his own philosophy is given always as vision.   He does not wrestle with Time, and conquer it : rather he takes the picture of Time flying.

The commentary of quotations running along the margins affords hints and clues : hints on interpretation or appreciation, clues to the sources from which the poem has sprung. In effect, the commentary reviews the poem more effectively than any sustained explanation.   For ' Time ' no matter how approached will not yield to scrutiny.   de la Mare darts at it, seems to have it fast, lets it go ; loves it, wants it, seeks it, loses it ; wonders at it, and never wastes it :

> *Were moments seeds, we then therein might say*
> *What hidden kind, hue, value, beauty lay,*
> *Virtue and quality.   But, these away,*
>
> *Theirs only quantity, mere measurement,*
> *Sans substance, pattern, form, shape, taste and scent—*
> *Flimsier than bubble, and more transient.*
>
> *Should, then, a Stranger from another Sphere*
> *Enquire, ' This Time, of which so much I hear ?*
> *Light-dark ; heat-cold ; void-solid : these are clear ;*
> *But TIME ?   What is it ?   Show me some, Monsieur ! '*

What should we choose for semblance ?   A flake of snow ?
A beach-brine bubble ?   A tiny shell or two ?
Poised in the sun, pure diamond of dew ?
Or whisper, ' Look ! a *clock !*   Now watch Time flow ;
It's a Machine, you see.   It makes it go *'*

Bland face; sly jerking hands :   staring he'd stay
Dumbly astonished.   And then turn, and say,
Closer to nothingness could nothing stray !
And now, pray, make Time flow the *other* way !

But clock-time, measured time, for de la Mare is the least part of the matter.   In its entirety the poem can be described as a sustained lyric of exceptional beauty ; it can be measured beside *Hero and Leander*, *Nymphidia*, *The Ancient Mariner*, or *Goblin Market*.

These two late flowerings of his genius apart, readers will always look to him first for the short lyrics which—any time in the past fifty years—have graced periodicals, anthologies, and, more recently, radio programmes.   Some of these poems are among the most widely known of our time, their opening lines familiar to all who care for poetry : 'Here lies a most beautiful lady', '" Bunches of grapes ", says Timothy', '" Is there anybody there ? " said the Traveller ', ' Who said, " Peacock Pie " ? ', ' What lovely things thy hand hath made '—and many more.   The poetry of our time does not always enter easily into the consciousness of millions ; these poems do so because they have a simplicity, a universality, which captures the reader at the outset and never lets him go.

WALTER DE LA MARE

A

Select Bibliography

(Place of publication London, unless stated otherwise)

Bibliographical Note :

The bibliography of Walter de la Mare's works in verse and prose is unusually complicated by the number and variety of the editions, issues and re-impressions in which they have been published, as well as by alterations in contents and text, in editions subsequent to the first. Some of the books in the following short-title list have also been published in illustrated editions, others in limited and unlimited issues. Almost all the author's verse and prose is available in one or other of the ' Collected Editions ' and ' Selections ' listed hereunder. The exceptions (not all of which are recorded here) are short prefaces and contributions to anthologies and books by other writers.

Collected editions :

POEMS, 1901–1918. 2 vols. (1920).

POEMS, 1919–1934 (1935).

COLLECTED POEMS (1942).

COLLECTED RHYMES AND VERSES (1944).
Light verse, nursery rhymes, jingles, etc.

COLLECTED STORIES FOR CHILDREN (1947).

Selections :

STORY AND RHYME (1921).

SEVEN SHORT STORIES (1931).
From *The Riddle, Broomsticks* and *The Connoisseur.*

OLD RHYMES AND NEW, 2 vols. (1932).
A selection of Walter de la Mare's verse chosen for use in schools.

THE WALTER DE LA MARE OMNIBUS (1933).
Containing the novels *Henry Brocken, The Return* and *Memoirs of a Midget.*

THE NAP AND OTHER STORIES (1936).
From *The Connoisseur* and other works, in the Nelson Classics.

STORIES, ESSAYS, AND POEMS (1938).
Selected by M. M. Bozman for Everyman's Library.

THE PICNIC (1941).
Selected prose in the Sesame Books Series.

TIME PASSES (1942).
Selected poems in the Sesame Books Series.

BEST STORIES OF WALTER DE LA MARE (1942).

Separate Works :

SONGS OF CHILDHOOD (1902). *Verse.*
See entry under ' Books for Children ' below. This title, and *Henry Brocken*, 1904, appeared under the name Walter Ramal.

HENRY BROCKEN (1904). *Novel.*

POEMS (1906). *Verse.*

THE RETURN (1910). *Novel.*
Revised 1922 and 1945.

THE LISTENERS AND OTHER POEMS (1912). *Verse.*

THE SUNKEN GARDEN AND OTHER POEMS (1917). *Verse.*

MOTLEY AND OTHER POEMS (1918). *Verse.*

RUPERT BROOKE AND THE INTELLECTUAL IMAGINATION (1919). *Lecture.*

FLORA : A Book of Drawings by Pamela Bianco (1919).
With illustrative poems by Walter de la Mare.

MEMOIRS OF A MIDGET (1921). *Novel.*

THE VEIL AND OTHER POEMS (1921). *Verse.*

CROSSINGS : A Fairy Play (1921). *Drama.*
With musical notes.

THE RIDDLE (1923). *Stories.*

THUS HER TALE, Edinburgh (1923). *Verse.*
A single poem, in the Porpoise Press Broadsides Series.

DING DONG BELL (1924). *Epitaphs,* with a commentary.

A BALLAD OF CHRISTMAS (1924). *Verse.*
A single poem in pamphlet form.

BROOMSTICKS (1925). *Stories.*

THE CONNOISSEUR (1926). *Stories.*

STUFF AND NONSENSE (1927). *Verse.*

ALONE (1927). *Verse.*
A single poem, in pamphlet form, in the Ariel Poems series.

SELF TO SELF (1928). *Verse.*
A single poem, in pamphlet form, in the Ariel Poems series.

A SNOWDROP (1929). *Verse.*
A single poem, in pamphlet form, in the Ariel Poems series.

NEWS (1930). *Verse.*
A single poem, in pamphlet form, in the Ariel Poems series.

ON THE EDGE (1930). *Stories.*

TO LUCY (1931). *Verse.*
A single poem, in pamphlet form, in the Ariel Poems series.

THE PRINTING OF POETRY, Cambridge (1931). *Essay.*

LEWIS CARROLL (1932). *Criticism.*
First published in *The Eighteen Eighties*, a series of essays by
Fellows of the Royal Society of Literature, edited by W. de la
Mare, 1930.

THE LORD FISH (1933). *Stories.*

THE FLEETING (1933). *Verse.*

A FROWARD CHILD (1934). *Story.*

THE WIND BLOWS OVER (1936). *Stories.*

POETRY IN PROSE (1936).
The Warton Lecture on English Poetry, British Academy 1935.

THIS YEAR, NEXT YEAR (1937). *Verse.*

MEMORY, AND OTHER POEMS (1938). *Verse.*

IN A LIBRARY (1938). *Verse.*

HAUNTED (1939). *Verse.*
A single poem, published as Linden Broadsheet No. 4.

PLEASURES AND SPECULATIONS (1940). *Essays.*
Including occasional critical papers ; *Rupert Brooke and the
Intellectual Imagination*, 1919 ; and *Poetry in Prose*, 1936.

BELLS AND GRASS (1941). *Verse.*

THE MAGIC JACKET AND OTHER STORIES (1943). *Stories.*

THE SCARECROW AND OTHER STORIES (1945).   *Stories.*

THE BURNING GLASS AND OTHER POEMS (1945).   *Verse.*

THE DUTCH CHEESE AND OTHER STORIES (1946).   *Stories.*

THE TRAVELLER (1946).   *Verse.*

CHARDIN, J. B. S.   1699–1779 (1948).   *Art.*
With Introduction and Notes by Walter de la Mare, in the
Faber Gallery Series.

INWARD COMPANION (1950).   *Verse.*

WINGED CHARIOT (1951).   *Verse.*

PRIVATE VIEW (1953).   *Criticism.*

Books for Children :

SONGS OF CHILDHOOD (1902).   *Verse.*
Published under the pen-name Walter Ramal.

THE THREE MULLA-MULGARS (1910).   *Story and Verse.*
Reprinted in 1935 as *The Three Royal Monkeys or The Three
Mulla-Mulgars* and in 1946 as *The Three Royal Monkeys.*

A CHILD'S DAY (1912).   *Verse.*

PEACOCK PIE (1913).   *Verse.*

DOWN-ADOWN-DERRY (1922).   *Verse.*

MISS JEMIMA.   Oxford (1925).   *Story.*

OLD JOE.   Oxford (1927).   *Story.*

LUCY.   Oxford (1927).   *Story.*

TOLD AGAIN.   Oxford (1927).   *Stories.*
Traditional tales re-told.

READINGS.   6 vols.   Oxford (1925–26).   *Stories.*
A series of traditional and other tales, Vols. I and II, told by
Walter de la Mare and Vols. III to VI chosen by him and
by Thomas Quayle.

POEMS FOR CHILDREN (1930).   *Verse.*

TOM TIDDLER'S GROUND (1932).   *Verse.*
An anthology of poetry for children.

THE OLD LION AND OTHER STORIES (1942).   *Stories.*
Published in the U.S.A. as *Mr. Bumps and His Monkey.*

Anthologies, Collections and Commentaries :

COME HITHER (1923). *Anthology and Commentary.*
Revised and enlarged 1928.

THE SHAKESPEARE SONGS (1929).
With an Introduction.

STORIES FROM THE BIBLE (1930). *Anthology.*

CHRISTINA ROSSETTI'S POEMS (1930).
With an Introduction.

DESERT ISLANDS (1930). *Anthology and Commentary.*

EARLY ONE MORNING IN THE SPRING (1935). *Anthology and Commentary.*
'Chapters on children and on childhood as it is revealed in particular in early memories and in early writings.'

ANIMAL STORIES (1939). *Anthology.*
Including many stories by Walter de la Mare.

BEHOLD THIS DREAMER (1939). *Anthology and Commentary.*

LOVE (1943). *Anthology and Commentary*

Some Studies and Appreciations :

WALTER DE LA MARE, by R. L. Mégroz (1924).

WALTER DE LA MARE, a Critical Study by Forrest Reid (1929).

POETRY AT PRESENT, by C. Williams (1930).
Includes a study of Walter de la Mare.

FIVE NOVELIST POETS OF TO-DAY, by R. L. Mégroz (1933).
Includes a study of Walter de la Mare.

EIGHT FOR IMMORTALITY, by R. Church (1941).
Includes a study of Walter de la Mare.

WALTER DE LA MARE, by J. Atkins (1947).

LIVING WRITERS, edited by G. Phelps (1947).
Includes a study of Walter de la Mare's stories by Dylan Thomas.

ESSAYS AND REFLECTIONS, by Harold Child (1948).
Includes a study of Walter de la Mare.

TRIBUTE TO WALTER DE LA MARE ON HIS 75TH BIRTHDAY (1948).
Contributors include Edmund Blunden, Lord David Cecil, Lord Dunsany, T. S. Eliot, Wilfred Gibson, Graham Greene, C. Day Lewis, John Masefield, Sir Edward Marsh, J. Middleton Murray, J. B. Priestley, V. Sackville West, Siegfried Sassoon.

WALTER DE LA MARE, by H. C. Duffin (1949).

[A SELECTION OF THE PROSE AND POETRY OF EDMUND BLUNDEN] (1950),
by K. Hopkins.
Includes a study of Walter de la Mare.

Messrs. Blackwell publish *Told Again* at 8s. 6d. net.

Messrs. Constable publish *Come Hither* at 15s. net.

Messrs. Dent publish *Stories, Essays and Poems* in Everyman's Library at 4s. 6d. net and *Story and Rhyme* at 1s. 10d. net.

Messrs. Faber and Faber publish *Behold this Dreamer* at 42s. ; *Early One Morning* and *Love* at 25s. net ; *Desert Islands* at one guinea net ; *Collected Poems*, 15s. ; *Collected Rhymes and Verses*, 12s. 6d. net ; *Stories from the Bible* at 15s. net ; *Animal Stories, Collected Stories for Children, Memoirs of a Midget* and *The Three Royal Monkeys* at 10s. 6d. ; *Chardin* at 9s. 6d. net ; *Best Stories, Inward Companion* and *Peacock Pie* at 8s. 6d. net ; *The Burning Glass, Bells and Grass, Songs of Childhood, Stuff and Nonsense*, and *The Traveller* at 7s. 6d. net ; *Crossings* at 6s. net ; *Ding Dong Bell, Henry Brocken, The Listeners, The Scarecrow* and *The Magic Jacket* at 5s. net ; *The Dutch Cheese* and *The Old Lion* at 4s. 6d. net.

The Oxford University Press publish *Poetry in Prose* at 5s. net.

Prices are liable to change and volumes to go out of print without notice.